BERRIES

CORA MCMILLAN

GUILDHALL PRESS

Published in September 2015

Guildhall Press
Ráth Mór Business Park
Derry, BT48 0LZ
Ireland
info@ghpress.com
www.ghpress.com
T: 028 7136 4413

Cover image © Eileen Deery, 2015.

Cover design by Kevin Hippsley.

ISBN: 978 1 911053 02 6

All proceeds from the sale of this book will go towards the Girl Rising project – the global campaign for girls' education in the developing world. (See www.girlrising.com for details.)

Working in conjunction with Sr Deirdre Mullan RSM, all proceeds will go to the provision of scholarships for the children of the Nuba, in Sudan, an isolated mountain region which is under constant attack and is the focus of ethnic cleansing by the government. Thank you for your support and action because it is not enough to be compassionate – we must ACT.

The Author

Cora McMillan was born in Creggan in 1955 and lives in Derry. She qualified as a teacher of English and Drama with a BA (Hons) and MEd, and taught in Notre Dame High School, London, and St Mary's College, Creggan. She is now retired.

McMillan has produced a number of musicals for St Mary's Musical Society and St Brigid's Musical Society: *Annie, The King and I* and *Oklahoma*, a community pageant in St Joseph's Church, Galliagh. She has led creative writing projects in community settings, edited Galliagh Women's Centre's publication *Dancers*, and has a number of individual poems published in *Fingerpost*, the *Derry Journal* and anthologies such as *Our Say, Snow in Summer* and *Writes of Spring*. Along with Moira Curran, she compiled *50 Golden Years* for the 50th anniversary of St Mary's College.

Cora McMillan has three adult children: Monica, Gráinne and James. This is her first poetry collection.

Acknowledgements

Thank you to my sisters, who have always encouraged me to write, and to my children Monica, Gráinne and James for their interest, IT know-how, advice and practical help.

A special thanks to Marilyn, Madeleine and Ellen – who took the time and interest to help these poems form and evolve – for their support and encouragement, especially in those critical self-doubting moments.

Thanks to Mary Murphy for her poetry evenings, the Shantallow Library Writers' Group and the Buncrana Writers' Group for their inspiration and feedback on this writing.

And my gratitude to Eamon and Paul and all at Guildhall Press for their support, encouragement and confidence in this work.

For Monica, Gráinne,
James and Chloe

CONTENTS

Stepping Out

Wilted silk levitates, inflates
in the breeze, candy stripes.
Ropes untied, weights released
that bind us to the earth.
We rise. This woven basket
carries us, Molly and me.
A flame blasts in our centre.

She steps out onto cloud.
Below, a crowd all mute.
I watch her falling.
No parachute
to catch the air.
I weakly wave goodbye.
I drift towards the sun
in an air balloon.

Love Sickness

Now I sigh for you.
Your kiss of wine,
the bitter fragrance
of myrrh and aloes,
the shade of the shepherd's tent
as he grazes his flock,
the cedar and the cypress.

Now I sigh for you.
The golden bracelets,
the silver earrings,
the necklaces of pearl,
my chains become adornments,
my labourer's basket now broken.
I yearn for you.

Now I sigh for you.
Outside the royal enclosure,
my repression, my compression
breathed out.
From your robes,
my hardness of heart
unfolded, yielding
and opening.
I await entrance to the feast.
Now I sigh for you.

Complaint to the Pope

Dear Frank,
You don't mind me calling you Frank.
Congratulations on your new post:
a sentinel for the poor.
Some years ago
I wrote to the Vatican,
even sent a poem.
I must complain,
I await a reply
and I am one of the poor.

I speculate
that they think I have lost it,
not the faith,
but with my reports of mystical experiences,
I thought to inspire possibilities
of my candidacy for sainthood.
Who now are the saint makers?

I speculate
that they didn't like my poem.
It spoke of insect life in the desert,
of a wasteland of straw women
and the slow baking of bread.
It is perhaps cliché.
Who now are the canon makers?

I speculate
they may think I am womanist,
with slippery ideas.

They have become old,
but for all these ancient years
I still await a reply.
Who garners wisdom from age and tradition?

I am dismayed, however:
the new does not bring in the new.
Am I complaining to the right person?

Privilege of Morning

Sitting beneath an early Sunday
the crescent moon dims,
topmost branches hum
in consecration
conducted by the breeze.
I am held up in prayer
still as that blade of grass.

My last morning
in the convent garden of Drumalis.
Sun blessed week!
I return to my own trees,
birch, laurel, red robin,
eucalyptus and the cotoneaster.
Her red berries, like drops of blood,
now only blossom at the root.
She has a dead look about her.
But I believe she will once more give
branches and berries.

Time and time ago in a church garden
of ripened strawberries, raspberries, gooseberries,
a butterfly landed on my skirt.
Red and blue and brown.
I see it in this stillness.
I watched with delight
as it held the white and green cotton.
A priest of creation,
who shone his shoes

on the calves of his trousers,
brushed the butterfly.
In the sudden separation,
my delight fled
as if I was unworthy
of the attention.
I spoke in a glance
but the priest did not answer.

Roses in this garden in Drumalis now fade.
Blossoming is certain next year,
performing an act of faith
in resurrection,
in the sun beyond the grey
and black dappled clouds.

A honey bee circles my head.
I content myself.
Soon I will make honey
with the beekeeping gardener.

We're Waiting for the Horse

Pressed between the couch
and the flock wallpaper,
toes straining to reach the sill,
net curtain tickles our necks,
we're waiting for the horse.
We're waiting for the horse.

He promised when the horse came up
he would come to our house.
We're waiting for the horse,
we're waiting for the horse.

This will be no cart-horse
with hairy boots and fat shanks,
of the milkman, fishman,
brockman, ragman,
but a Black Beauty,
a steed of Lochinvar,
steaming muscles,
cavernous nostrils,
sycamore ears.
We're waiting for the horse.

The sun winks, falls laughing
behind the roofs of the terraced houses
mocking our wait.
We linger.
We have been promised.
The swinging gate is waiting.
We're waiting for the horse.

Expecting the council estate
to make a bum's rush to our street
for the spectacle,
we're waiting for the horse.
Round the corner, him on a bicycle.
No hooves on the pavement or tar,
just his flat cap down against the wind.
No horse.

The soles of our feet
slap the floor.
Where's the horse, Granda?
You promised when the horse came up
you would come.

The horse did come up.
Fifty to one.

Under Observation

'How do you know I am mad?' said Alice.
'You must be,' said the cat, 'or you wouldn't have come here.'
(Alice's Adventures in Wonderland, *Lewis Carroll*)

Sleepless,
I shift along the silent ward and corridor.
He sits behind the desk.
A single lamp on papers or porn?
The monitor flickers down.

He leans as I turn the corner.
On the screen above
my silken red pyjamas
drift across the polished floor.
Leaving his station, he takes me to a room
that doesn't exist,
makes me tea and toast.

I hear the hobble of the crutches,
a girl who poured paraffin,
now stirred from blistered sleep.
She pours a cup of tea
with bandaged hands.

We dream of the river
of Foyle Search and Rescue,
a schizophrenic city,
the Peace Bridge.
We drink our virtual tea.

I watch the night nurse boil the kettle.
Another cup of tea.
He wears his badge of sanity.
Without a uniform
he is still in charge.
His smile betrays his crooked teeth.

I know this girl from school.
Real books
monitoring and evaluating
testing and targets.
This low-lit gloom
casts shadows on our eyes.
We speak in whispers,
drink tea, eat toast
and return to our observation posts.

This night-time kindness.

To What Can I Lay Claim?

Honeydew scents of snuff
remind me of her presence.
A childhood message
to Blutcher Street
for a shilling's worth in a paper cone.
The brown-stained hankie
bulging in her apron pocket.

Another errand to the long grasses
of the rear yard,
hunting for a spray of shepherd's purse
to feed her caged budgies.

I did not know her
in the flywheels,
furls of cotton and linen,
spores dusting the air,
mechanical beats of sewing trills,
dry vibrations of the shirt factory.

I did see her bent
with the black polish
smelling of paraffin,
smutching and buffing the range,
her rump swinging
in her solitary dance.

I was allowed at her elbow,
a story for each sepia image.
Singing in a choir
in the Guildhall Square.

A boy-uncle I mistook for my brother
on the Breakneck Steps.
Her wedding.
Her man on a bicycle.

In her grey fading
she carried her crippled man
up and down the stairs
till she buried him.

I held a candle as we prayed.
She asked, *How long does it take to die?*
I ask my granny,
To what can I lay claim?

Inch Island Pier

A warm sun dropped light
between us. Wandering the pier
we did not stand in each other's shade.
Lough Swilly smiled.

Our usual trawlers had gone.
The empty lobster pots missing.
In our haven, moored tightly,
a little boat named Hopeful.

Her green and white paint stripped,
exhausted by the North Sea,
the chain of her anchor
shrank into black water.

She winked in the waves,
wrapped in her ropes.
She was safe.

Autumn Half-Term

I watch them from my window,
two children: a boy and a girl.
They dance in the puddles,
talk in their childish ways
without pester.
The young girl's ponytail swishes
with her leaps and runs.
The young boy watches.
They are happy.

The trampoline has stood
in a neighbour's garden,
a monument, deserted all summer,
now drips in the rain.
These children climb.
They hold hands and jump
as memories do.
All too soon, bored
they fall on to wet grass.

They disappear through a gate
to hot chocolate and teacakes.

Happy Christmas

Fifteen years in the waiting room,
looking through the mirror,
to the snow underfoot
of that December morning,
waiting for the shop to open:
a Saturday job
that earned me one pound for the day,
that cool crisp morning.
A foot patrol trudged
up Butcher Street.
I stood in the doorway.

A soldier, seventeen, no more,
in green khaki, in his hands
a rifle with night sights,
to kill in the dark,
a soldier who may have
broken down our doors,
torn up our floorboards,
tortured our fathers and brothers,
a soldier the same age as me,
stopped beside me in the doorway
and said *Happy Christmas*.
I turned away.

In the mirror,
John Young lies in his coffin,
a bullet hole, round and clean
at his nose, looks at me
with his white face.

The blackness of the hole
swallows me.
I turned away
from that Happy Christmas.

Now a soldier away from home,
a teenager in a lost Christmas.
Now World War One
in the horrors of mud and gas,
he plays football, sings *Silent Night*,
a Christmas Day ceasefire.
I turned away.

Our Father, lead us not into temptation.
Do not put us to the test.
What did you do during the war?
I turned away.

Now the waiting room. And him?
Afghanistan? A general?
Retired? Married with children?
Dead?

The door opens from December night rain.
An old woman enters the waiting room.
She has come to pray, to grieve,
her husband only dead a month.
She weeps *I hope he is in heaven*
We talk. We pray. We sit in silence.
We are friends.
We have our secrets.

Her husband, a paratrooper,
retired to live in his enemy's territory,
in fear of discovery.
A marksman.
She is the Christmas gift to me.
I hope he is in heaven too.

Together she and I pray
to all the soldiers of the world.
May the Christ child be born in you.
Happy Christmas.

Empty Nest Syndrome

We went to honour Heaney,
read *Anahorish,* the death of *Beowulf,*
Mary Heaney at the graveside.
The *fluttering flowers* of Ledwidge
crowned the clay.
Red berries of autumn
overhung the drystone wall.
We stopped in the unpoetic church.
The others lit candles, said prayers.
At the back, beside me in the pew,
an abandoned soother,
clear rubber on yellow plastic,
a red ribbon.
A tear escaped.

Confession

Bless me Father for I have sinned.
It is two years since my last confession.
I smoke.

So smoking's a sin now! Is it?
He lit up.
His cloud issued through the door
to the crowded oratory.

Do you give to the poor?
A sharp red glow.
Yes.
How much?
I don't know.
I inhaled.
Do you have children?
Yes.
Are they on drink or drugs?
After-tails of smoke rose in the dark.
Have you stolen? Told lies?
He growled louder
till the interrogation burned.

My feet arched at the starting block
ready to run.
Where's your father and mother?
They're both dead. They smoked.
What about your friends?
I don't have any. I smoke.
Have you killed anyone?
Just myself.

I exhaled.
Our Lady, Queen of confessors,
pray for us.

In forty years I have never heard
a confession like this.

We were both far gone.
Did I give you absolution?
I don't know.
Away with you!

Christina's City of Culture

With bleached beehive, she wore
her belted raincoat too short
for her tweed skirt.

When it was sunny
she stood in Foyle Street
at a bus stop.
She stood in the Guildhall Square
outside the Post Office.

When it was raining,
she stood in Tescos and Superfare,
in Boots and Sainsburys.
She couldn't stand in Dunnes
once they asked her what was wrong.
In Austins, they offered her a chair.

When she had stood too long,
she sat in Ramsey's
with one cup of coffee
and a newspaper she couldn't read.

Familiar faces spoke to her.
Not remembering their names,
she pretended, in a rush, to smile.

She sweated in The Void,
trembled in Superbowl,
walked the Peace Bridge,
stared at the river.

A Black & Decker in B & Q
made her cry.
When it was dark she went home.

Second Chance

A bee punched in my open window,
a motorbike round my living room.
It rested on my knee.
A memory of a five-year-old,
a sting on my bum.
I squashed the bee
with the holy book in my hand.

It was not vengeance, just fear.
I thought I could kill anything.
Black, its delicate wings fanned,
a stain of blood.

A queen bee in Spring.
I wept for the bee,
for the hive,
for myself,
as I swept it into the bin.

Friends consoled me,
examined the bee in the bin.
It wasn't really a queen.
It wasn't really a honey bee.
Just a bumble bee.
Just a bee.
I knew the truth.
I saw it dead.

Time later, another bee
struck through my open window.

With glass and card,
I trapped it.

Outside with arms raised,
in the ritual moment
of letting go,
my second chance,
it hovered.
A windswept freedom.
The forgiveness of the bees.

Mount Tabor

Onward and upward.
Wings of the wind turn from the North,
circling. Handholds and footholds
precarious in the cold blast. A birth.
Moments' shelter in caves
of nothing, nothing, nothing.
Mouth's thirst for sunlight.
Begin a self-comforting humming.
Follow the track of some mountain goat
in an unknown ascent.
No ropes or harness. Sweat-soaked.
A descent into the soul.
A wide ledge opens to rest
bathed in hot sun till bleached,
attack by an eagle defending her nest.
Running now to a summit never reached.
Up and down. Up and down,
off balance with the heat, lack of oxygen.
Hallucinating. Light white robes flowing.
Dazzling, parched. Ten
thousand beams blinding. Then night
falls and still in starlight
I stand on a crescent moon
wait, hear the summit call.
Shall I unroll a tent?
Too quickly now descend.
Was it a trick of the mind
lived in imagination
deep in memory's well
of a story remembered?

A Tree and the Wind in Early Spring

I was in disagreement with him
in the depth of winter.
He had scattered my flock of leaves.
But now the ground is wiped dry
with a warm spring breath.

The wind wears a death mask
in the early morning
putting my suspicions to sleep.
I stretch out my branches.

But if I should put forth leaves,
he would still rise up
with a vengeance
to play the devil
with my spring dewdrops.

A Passing Grief

Reeds on the horizon bend in an arc.
Bees have deserted the hive.
An aspen trembles, grey violets droop.
A lost sparrow on a leafless twig.
Ruins of a medieval abbey black in the skyline.

Once free-flying geese could be heard,
fiddle and harp in a parish hall.
Once perfumed turf from thatch and half-door.

Now the heaped stones,
a headstone's rhythm and rhyme broken,
a grotto of chipped blue and white paint
where travellers leave ribbons, beads, photographs,
debris of remembrances.

Our Lady of Sorrows weeps.
Long shadows mark the time of day.
Light and dark play tricks.
In a summer sunset, all would look different.
Do not think poor of me.

Guardian of the Threshold – He Weku

You hang above the door
with your metal eyeballs
in glistening shell eyes
and your tongue sticking out.
Not just defiance but magic
to circle this home
with meetings and greetings
of those who dare to pass.

A warning to intruders or evil forces
of an imaginary monster
that lies within.
For those gentle souls,
who have visited before,
who know of myth and art,
of the hearth and fire,
there is some protection.

Stay Away: Advice to a Teenage Daughter

Stay away from *The Virgin and the Gypsy*,
DH Lawrence in general.
Stay away from TS Eliot
and *Sweeney Among the Nightingales*.
It will do you no good.

Stay away from ex-soldiers,
priests, milkmen, postmen, teachers,
men with dogs who name them Dog.
They have no imagination.

Stay away from bullets and barricades,
petrol bombs and guns.
They lead to death and prison.

Stay away from those friends
at the back of the playground
who have enough money
to buy a packet of ten.
It's easy to share.

Stay away from those risky ideas
like waterfall climbing
or rock climbing at the Devil's Hole
without ropes.
It's amazing you're still alive.

Stay away from people who wear costumes
for photographs on Christmas cards.
They don't know who they are.

Stay away from long evenings in pubs
with people you don't know.
You'll be left to find your own way home.

Stay away.

Tigers in Creggan

Up behind the Cropie
lives a tiger
near the reservoir,
lives silently
in the forest.

Green and black striped,
it crouches in the night,
near the water's edge
to sip
and sometimes terrify
the glue-sniffers in the pipe.

Lonely women travelling to Glenowen
at night
know the tiger
but never speak of it
to anyone

For fear

of being accused
of drinking in the Telstar
of being *bad with the nerves*
of being *in that time of life*
of being talked about

in muted whispers
over cups of tea
in sunlit kitchens

while husbands swank in Saudi
or the bookies
or drink in the Telstar.

Ruhamah in the Resurrection Garden

Before the altar,
preparing the diorama
of that Easter morning,
I kneel on the soft carpet steps.
How often I have tried
to construct with block board
the many stage sets
for those play productions.
Now, with artist's knife,
I slide easily through
to form the cave-tomb
in three dimensions.

Burnt sienna, yellow ochre,
my favourite hard-edged
paintbrush forms
rock-shaped sand dunes.
Filling in with dark brown,
those shadows I own:
the backdrop of a desert.
Some grey to line a tomb door,
(some things are not black and white),
scattered rocks around the entrance.
Acrylic paints dry in seconds,
as layer upon layer is dabbed on.

I staple the sheet of death's black silk
inside the door,
cut a neat strip of life's white linen
to lie across this tomb-block,

(some things are black and white).
Now a stone I once uncovered
by the sea, made smooth
by rock and salt,
rolls to rest against the cave,
reveals the entrance
to the empty tomb.
A surviving witness.

Neatly showing
Spring plants in flower,
seated on slate stones,
now bloom red, yellow, black
pink and white
against this sandy hill.
Delicately,
two satin-winged birds
both alight,
a moment's life
suspended,
waiting for the wind.

Ruhamah carries in
the jar of Arabian perfumed oil.
I arise.

Ruhamah: Hebrew: beloved, she who has obtained mercy

Owl's Feather

Here an owl's feather, gift from Shirley Bear,
Medicine woman, caretaker of the earth
from the Bear Tribe Reservation.
Ancient mound builders of Cahokia,
they walked across an ice-age bridge,
hunters of sloth the size of buffalo,
armadillos the size of buses,
woolly mammoth.
They gathered maize and beans and squash.
Basket makers of the Navajo,
astronomers, builders, traders, potlatch gift givers,
carvers of totem poles, birch bark canoes.
Mohawks, Lakota, Apache, Hopi,
Choctaws, Chickasaws, Cherokee, Cheyenne.
Drumbeat in the silence.

An exotic species in a strange new world,
the Sword, the Cross and Smallpox.
Convert or die! And died in fear of going
to heaven to meet only Christians there.
Cabot, Columbus, Hudson, Balboa,
Magellan, Drake, Raleigh, Verrazano.
Massacred in the silence.

Here a remnant – an owl's feather.
God speaks one Word.
He speaks in the silence.

This solitary feather deserving honour,
brown, tan, black velvet.

Owl camouflage, upright in his roost,
binocular light-gathering eyes,
swivelling head, depends on stealth,
endangered, protected even in death,
slow in the silence.

This feather, gifted for courage
beaded for my hair, from the owl
who skims in the night
in wisdom, in forgiveness
in the silence.

Roots

This embryonic seedling
is held by a radicle.
This sliver becomes the tap root
diving down into the dark,
only to die so early.

Lateral roots, crowned with hair,
branch out, search
through mud,
shy away from dryness,
sense each obstacle,
grow strong enough
to burst water pipes,
crack concrete.

Above the wind blows.
A thin trunk sways.
Below, cells break, divide.
Vegetation welds.
Nodules form
till buttresses flare
out from the trunk,
anchoring angle brackets.

Vascular tissue heals,
thickens the diameter
after those many breaks,
till cherry tree stands rooted,
till she flowers and fruits,
despite the storms.
Real roots grow
through brokenness and death.

Photographer's Gaze

That's my last Duchess painted on the wall,
Looking as if she were alive.
(My Last Duchess, Ferrara, *Robert Browning*)

Da takes photos of me
in waves,
short, shallow waves,
at the edge of the sea.

Behind my shadows
glows the evening sun,
reflected
in the salt sea.

Dusk stretches
beyond the waves,
towards my da,
knees deep in soft sand.

Camera lens
captures
my little girl's curls.
I am caught forever

between the sun
and his gaze.

China Doll

Six-year-old's sea-sand hand
on Daddy's driving shoulder.
Bridin sings *Beautiful Bundoran*
knowing all the words.
Safely home, sisters
to summer's bed.
Daddy names her
his little China Doll.

Invisible in a green fog
the sisters watch.
Daddy sings
Sweet Sixteen.

With gas and stones,
Bridin sings
The Boys of Wexford.
Daddy doesn't sing.

Winter night, his China Doll
isn't home.

Whistling bullets stud the sky.
Gun battles gorge the hours,
Daddy flares the floor,
and sisters watch
a dawn-sky night of fires,
as the frozen sound
of china fingers turn the key.

Angry father feet
shut the family door,
as sisters hear
porcelain smashing
on the hall floor.

Coastguard

'Never swim unaccompanied in the sea' – Water Safety
Guidelines

My sister swims in sea.
A watery sun
fizzles through grey,
on that familiar red
plastic swimming cap.

Blackened seaweed
hugs her hips,
breast strokes
pulsing
to that rock
and back.

On our Donegal beach,
under a northern cloud,
I glimpse her bobbing,
thread gold orange sand
on her bath sheet.
I keep guard.

Riddle

We walked out to the bay, all the way,
past the bee on the pink honeysuckle
and the wild rose cup pointing skywards.
We hurried on, alive in the still air.
We climbed over rocks down to the wet sand,
where the remains of a dead crab lay,
the shell cracked open. No more side-stepping.
We wondered at the emptiness.
A wave licked the crunched claw tips, recoiling,
foaming at the mouth of the hollow crust.
The hidden sun danced a varnish
on vacant vitals, as froth filled the void.
We smiled at the riddle, at each other,
and laughed with the roar and sweep of the sea.

Remote Control

Ma's funeral afternoon,
in our barn at the back
of our house,
I'm on the unemployed couch.
A loo chain hangs on a hook,

a green blade of grass
in black gunge in a crock,
a dead stove,
where my da once burned to dust
my *Virgin and the Gypsy*.

I slip behind the cushions:
a stolen shilling, dried peas,
my thumb on
broken rosary beads
held by a nappy pin.

Dropping into a black hole,
daring a touch of ants
nesting in the springs.
That lost remote control.
I light a cigarette.

A casual flick
of a burning match.

Sister

No mirror was needed
until the day
you went to school
and I stayed at home.

Mother made you
the green pinafore
with shiny ebony buttons.
None for me.

I watched her dress you
that morning,
me, barefoot, in pyjamas,
you in patent black shoes.

I remember
your first day at school.
I don't remember
my own.

The Waiting Room

Steamed up windows on a rainy day,
a distant flash from the bridge,
a slow flap of flags,
I smudge the condensation
to see through the drops of water:
a river pilot guides a yacht
through the currents to the pier.

Baskets of wilting begonias
hang from the lamppost.
The clock ticks on the wall.
A magazine with promises,
Aphrodite's temples of beauty,
tempt from the low table.

I slip into my history
of Radio Four, the newspaper,
a cappuccino, a croissant.
I am released into the future
of the school run, of cooking dinner.
I must remember to shop for food.

The clock ticks, now reflected
in the misty glass.
A pigeon arrives on the sill,
pecks at the concrete but does not delay.
The begonias drip. Moments' events.

My eyes move
to the warm musty air.
My appointment may not be today.

Return

With an inappropriate rake
and orange wellies,
she stirred the sludge
from the bottom of the pond,
till the water clouded and blackened.

Hidden by a tree
in the prayer garden,
I watched her intention
to clear the swamp.

Rotting twigs and leaves
twined the prongs.
She bucketed the slop.
A recent dug channel
drained the effluent
to the roots of nearby trees.

She surveyed the remains.
Despite the horror,
with pink rubber gloves
and stained waterproofs,
she swept with a wire brush,

bucketing and bucketing,
till only grit was left
and tiny insects.
The sun baked the ground,
while a hose crawled on its belly
gurgling clear water.

Arctic Family Circle

My sister's gone to the Arctic Circle.
The baby of the family.
My mother told her to take plenty of clothes.
My older sister told her
she should come to Derry
and not be traipsing off,
hammering at rocks.

Ice caps are melting.
What could she find, under snow?
Experience and geography tell me
there's too much snow.

My older sister told my mother
she wouldn't have room for warm clothes
in her rucksack,
what with her hammer and chisel
hanging out
from her sack of tools,
to mine the Arctic Circle.

Ice-caps melt.
She'll drown under melting ice.
She shall have to swim,
to mine snow.

My brother told my sister
she was wasting her time
looking under snow.
She would find more snow.

My mother told me
she left this morning,
that I couldn't write to her.
She left no forwarding address.

Stress

Beep, Beep, Beep, Beep.
Sainsbury's own brand of cornflakes
passed along the belt.
Beep, Beep, Beep, Beep.

Tut, Tut, Tut, Tut.
She stood at my shoulder,
hopping from one foot to another.
Tut, Tut, Tut, Tut.

Ahem, Ahem, Ahem, Ahem.
She was in a hurry,
weighed down by her wire basket.
Ahem, Ahem, Ahem, Ahem.

A bread knife stuck
through the wire.
She now wept blood
from her wrists.

Beep, Beep, Beep, Beep.
Tut, Tut, Tut, Tut.
Ahem, Ahem, Ahem, Ahem.

Mia

Little brother had a doll
when he was fair and two.
Mia-doll was black,
black as navy-blue.

White father cursed the doll,
raged at the other
who'd given his heir
a doll for play.
The ram might be a wether.

His nappied son enfolded Mia
in his skittled arms,
wetting with the slabber
of his mother kiss
black rubber doll-lips.

Father despaired.

Did father take Mia
and break her
into pieces?
Father smiled.
Little brother cried,
as he held the arms,
bundled the head
with its black curls
and sockets wanting legs.
He hid her
in his armpit.

Little brother
now bigger,
black with Guinness,
muscled and angry,
darker than Mia
ever was.

Queen Anne Chair

'O happy dagger!
This is thy sheath; there rust and let me die.'
(Romeo and Juliet)

So chair,
your polished carvings
grip me, velvet
tickling my neck.

So chair,
you pull him to me,
knife drawn out.
Pillow me forward.

So chair,
you hold me up.
Spine sinking into plush,
wood burning my palms.

O chair,
Let me not die bitter.
With dagger at my throat,
his eyes are lakes.

O chair,
you see his steps,
slow, stockinged
on red carpet.

O chair,
your gift to me.
I speak, *If you're going out
put on your shoes.*

O chair,
velvet
tickling my neck
he turns away.

O chair,
you swallow me
in your cushion,
as he leaves.

Writing Disturbed by a Fly

It arrived – that indefinite article
after my ellipsis on toast and cup of colon,
flying round my head, the word buzzing
entered by the brackets of the window.
Swatting commas, hoping it will pause
so I can put a wordless glass
around it with unlined card
to rub it outside in the air.
My pen marches, its wings across the page
paying no heed to commas, colons or ellipsis,
line breaks or rhyme,
just searching for the full stop.

Daddy

Maple, pine, oak.
Stream-shredded sawdust
swish around my ankles
beside your handsaw.
Small wood off-cuts
are my childhood blocks,
while you make doors and frames.

You point a proud-perfect dovetail joint,
explain the maths,
as I play at your feet
in the wood perfume of your workshop.

The too-big-tree you did not saw
stands in our living room.
I know this is Christmas.

You leave your wood and trees,
go to work on the roads.
I leave my childish ways
take to the road.
You look for me
till I come back.
We talk into the night.
That perfect dovetail joint.

Mercy

He came towards me,
my lover.
Together we held
the tension
between love and hate.
He bore the bottle
of perfumed oil
worth half a million pounds
and poured it over me.
Every last drop.

Spring Grace

Spring bestows yellow blooms –
Winter Aconite and Witch Hazel,
purple favour of Crocus,
pale blueness of Glory of the Snow.
Benevolence of spring blossoms –
Lenten Rose, Camellia,
blue and white starry Anemones,
Peonies, Pansy, Primrose,
Star Magnolia, Lilac, Lily of the Valley,
Pussy Willow catkins and Iris
turn to the returning sun.
Blessings flow from hedgerows and gardens
without cost, gifts of Spring,
generous to the senses –
their only purpose to be beautiful.
Delight of a solitary nesting queen bee,
each flower expresses her divine self
in the dance of spring grace.

Praise for *Berries*

Cora McMillan's poems are at times touchingly tender, at other times quirky, unexpected and provocative. All the time, a questing spiritual energy ranges through her work. Her poetry explores themes of family, prayer, the Troubles and relationships against a background of life in Derry. She pays tribute to the women of Derry in her poem *To What Can I Lay Claim?* and through the lens of time reflects with humour and sadness on life and loss. These 'berries' offer an invitation to pick and ponder.

All the complexities and perplexities of life are unflinchingly faced, explored and deplored. These poems are brave and honest, also finely honed and crafted. Like well-tempered steel, they have a cutting edge. They are full of the authority of time and place, with a pure beauty and elegance of vivid, living, colloquial considered language. The simplicity and vigour of image, narrative and voice belie the shimmering, challenging and sometimes shocking depths of the poems – often shocking in a positive and emotionally enriching way – as if there is always the gentle admonition: 'Pause here, dwell with this image, this word, what resonates here?'

These poems have grown out of intellectual rigour and a clear-eyed drive for the truth. They are full of humour and mischief, challenge and compassion and an unfailing love for life. This is her debut collection and without doubt, there is more to come.

Marilyn McLaughlin, Author

***

I have greatly enjoyed, and wholeheartedly recommend, Cora's expansive *Berries* collection. The language delights from the very first lines of *Stepping Out*: '*Wilted silk levitates, inflates/in the breeze, candy stripes...*' to the endings which startle and delight as in *Return*: '*... a hose crawled on its belly gurgling clear water*'.

There are graphic portraits of characters made memorable in the writing. *China Doll* is a novel in a nutshell. Throughout, the poems are astute observations of the quotidian personal revelations, surreal treats and poignant challenges, like the profoundly redemptive *Happy Christmas*. These poems are accessible, often humorous, sometimes disturbing. And never dull.

James King, Performance poet

***

These poems are for anyone – whether you like poetry or not. Sadness and humour intertwine. An insightful collection.

Galliagh Women's Centre